PIANO · VOCAL · CHORDS

Idols' Top 10 Hits

With Sing-a-long Backing Tracks

T0040912

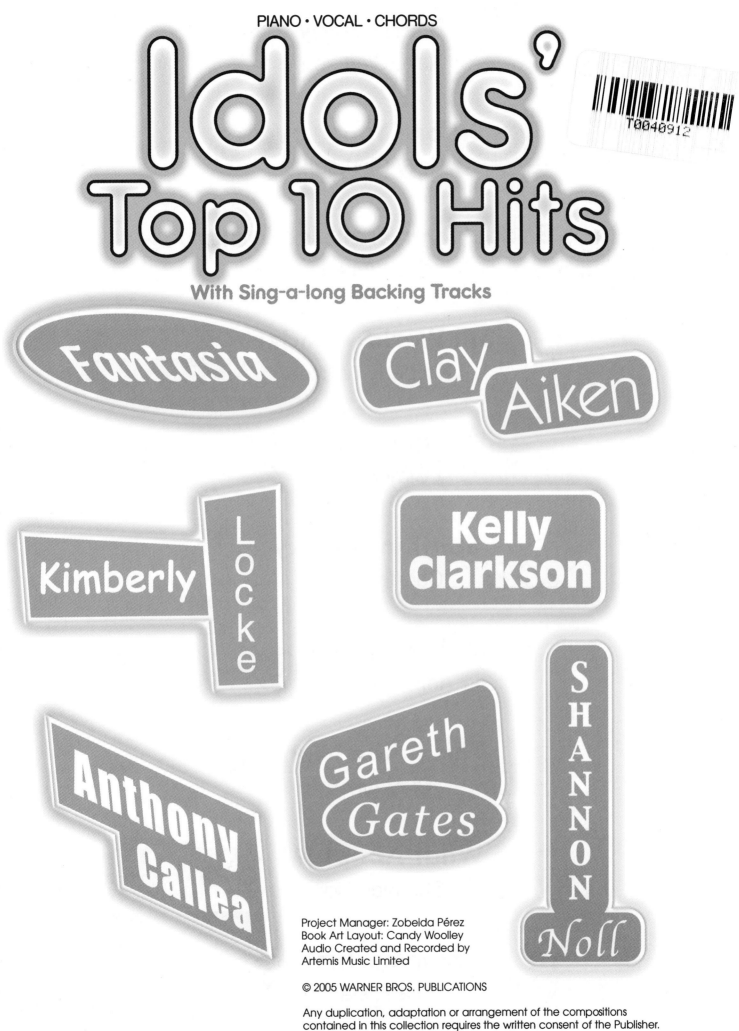

Fantasia

Clay Aiken

Kimberly Locke

Kelly Clarkson

Anthony Callea

Gareth Gates

SHANNON Noll

Project Manager: Zobeida Pérez
Book Art Layout: Candy Woolley
Audio Created and Recorded by
Artemis Music Limited

BREAKAWAY

Words and Music by
MATTHEW GERRARD, AVRIL LAVIGNE
and BRIDGET BENENATE

Moderately slow ♩. = 56

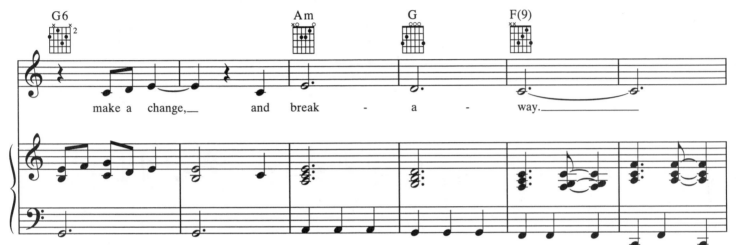

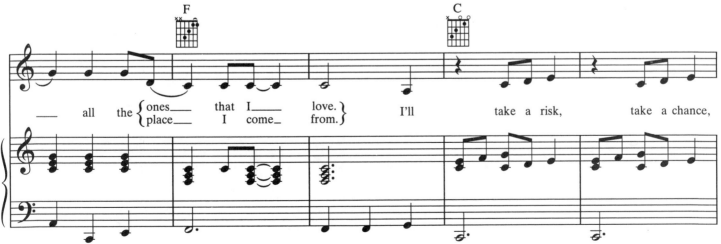

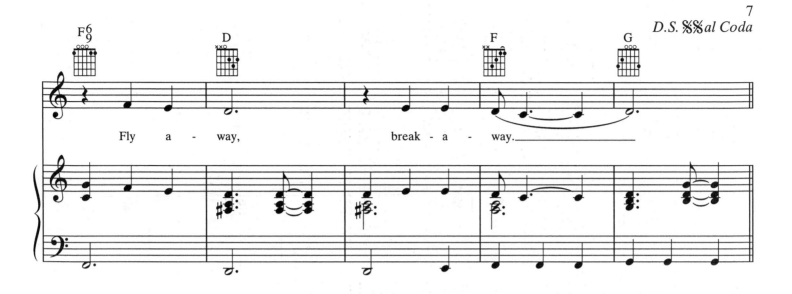

Fly a - way, break - a - way._____

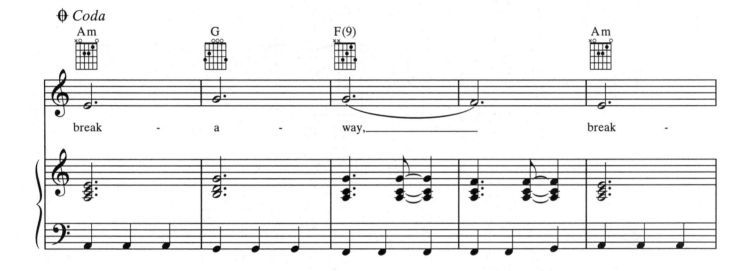

break - a - way,_____ break -

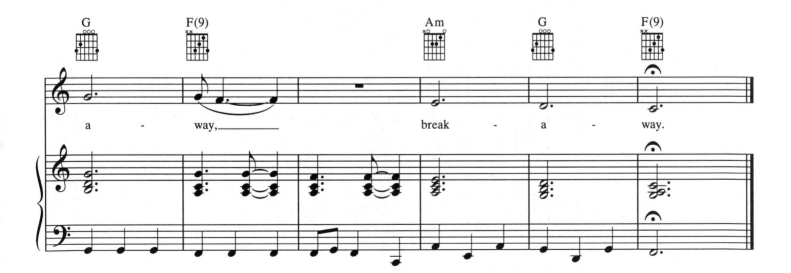

a - way,_____ break - a - way.

BEFORE YOUR LOVE

Words and Music by
DESMOND CHILD, GARY BURR
and CATHY DENNIS

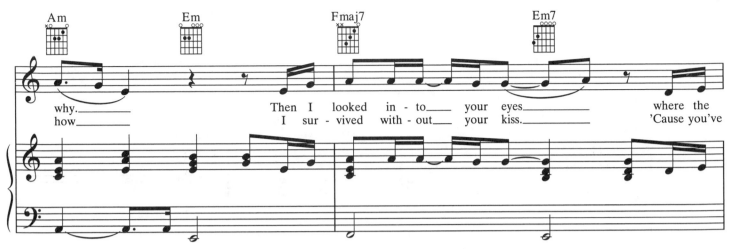

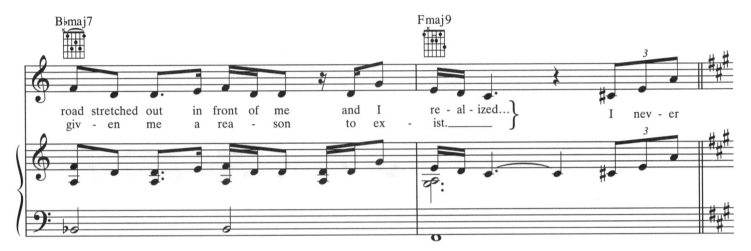

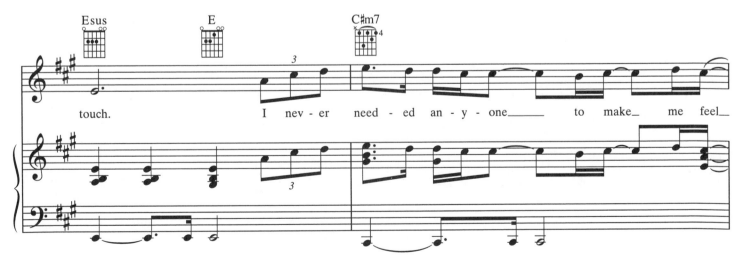

To Coda ⊕

a - live. But, then a - gain, I was - n't real - ly liv - ing. I nev - er

1.

lived be - fore your love.

2.

fore your love. I nev - er lived

be - fore your love.

And I don't know why,_____ why the

sun de-cides_ to shine,_____ but you breathed your love in-to me just in time.__ I nev-er

D.S. ℅ al Coda

Coda

lived,_____ I nev-er lived_____ be - fore_____ your_

love._____

BRIDGE OVER TROUBLED WATER

Words and Music by
PAUL SIMON

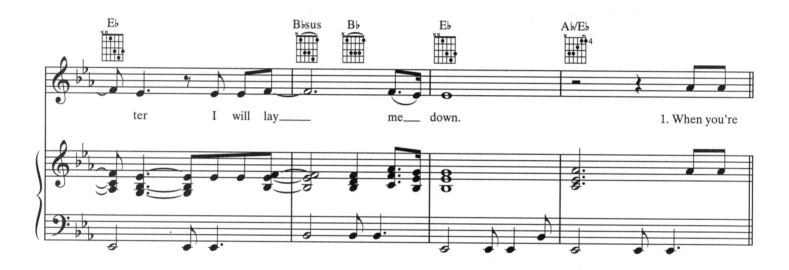

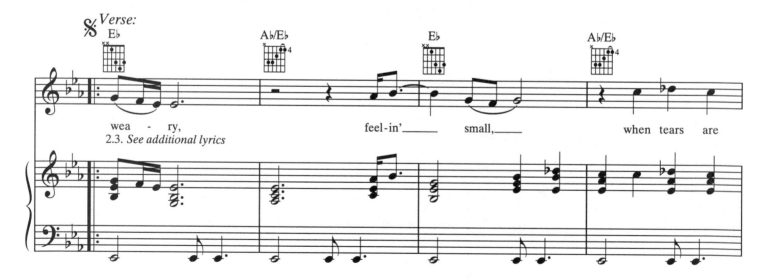

2. When you're

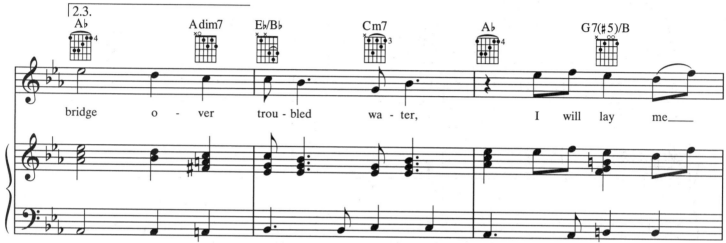

bridge o - ver trou - bled wa - ter, I will lay me____

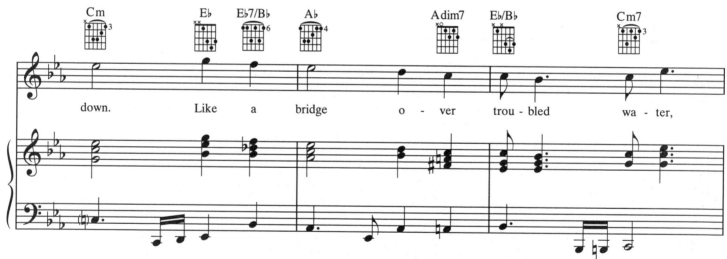

down. Like a bridge o - ver trou - bled wa - ter,

To Coda

I will lay me down.____

Verse 2:
When you're down and out,
When you're on the street,
When evening falls so hard, I will comfort you.
I'll take your part, oh, when darkness comes
And pain is all around.
Like a bridge over troubled water, I will lay me down.
Like a bridge over troubled water, I will lay me down.

Verse 3:
Sail on, silver girl, sail on by.
Your time has come to shine,
All your dreams are on their way.
See how they shine, oh if you need a friend,
I'm sailing right behind.
Like a bridge over troubled water, I will ease your mind.
Like a bridge over troubled water, I will ease your mind.

8TH WORLD WONDER

Words and Music by
KYLE JACOBS, SHAUN SHANKEL
and JOEL PARKES

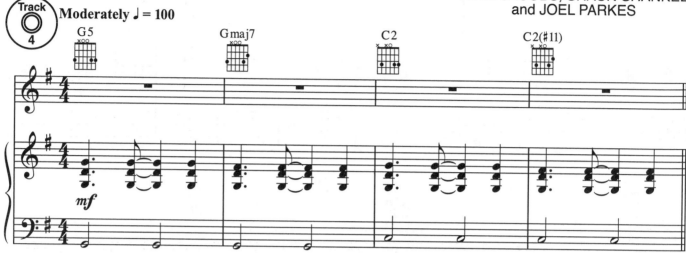

Verse:

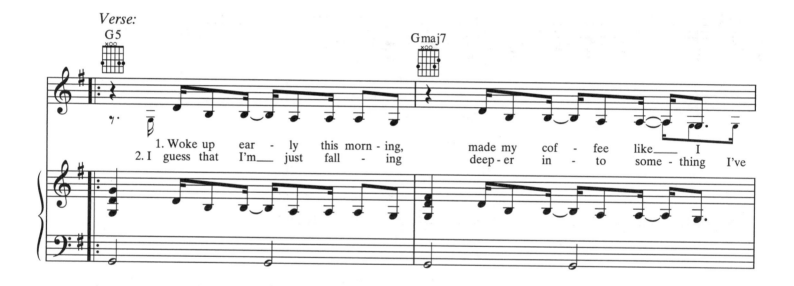

1. Woke up ear - ly this morn - ing, made my cof - fee like I
2. I guess that I'm just fall - ing deep - er in - to some - thing I've

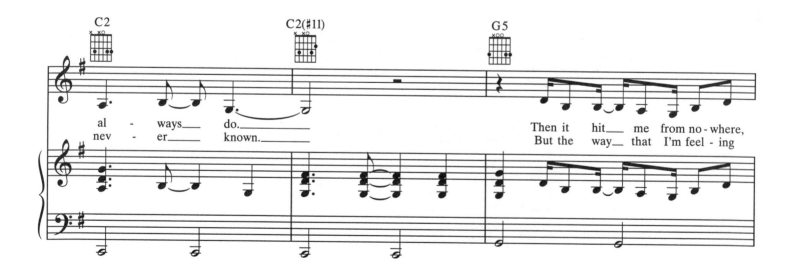

al - ways do.
nev - er known.

Then it hit me from no - where,
But the way that I'm feel - ing

8th World Wonder - 5 - 1
MFM0501CD

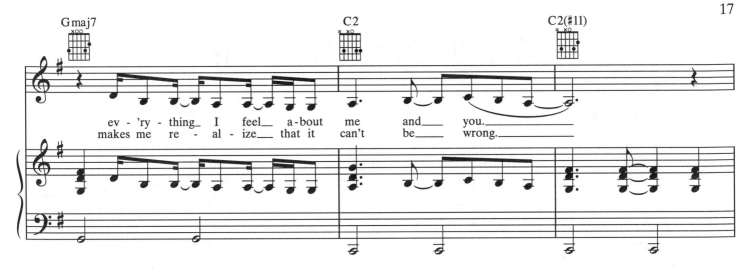

Chorus:

8th World Wonder - 5 - 2

MFM0501CD

...end solo)

Chorus:

Sev - en days_ and sev - en nights_ of thun - der. The wa - ter's ris - ing and I'm_

_ slip - ping un - der. I think I fell in love____ with the eighth_ world won -

der._____ Yeah,___ yeah, yeah,___ yeah. ___ yeah,___ yeah.___

20

Sev-en days and sev-en nights of thun-der. The wa-ter's ris - ing and I'm....

I think I fell in love with the eighth world won -

der. Hey, yeah, hey,

oh, yeah.

INVISIBLE

By CHRISTOPHER KENNETH BRAIDE,
ANDREAS MICHAEL CARLSSON and DESMOND CHILD

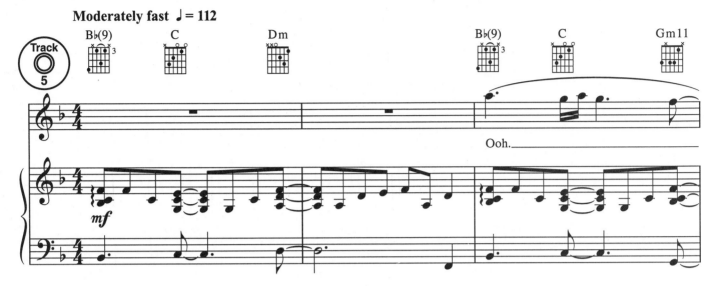

Ooh._____

Verse:

1. What — cha do-in' to-night?___ I wish I could be___
2. Saw your face in the crowd,___ I called out your name,___

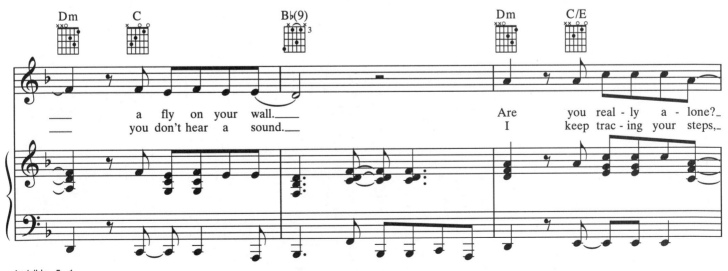

___ a fly on your wall.___ Are you real-ly a-lone?___
___ you don't hear a sound.___ I keep trac-ing your steps,___

Invisible - 5 - 1
MFM0501CD

SPIRIT IN THE SKY

Words and Music by
NORMAN GREENBAUM

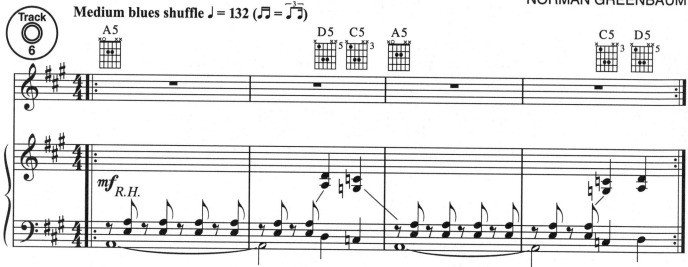

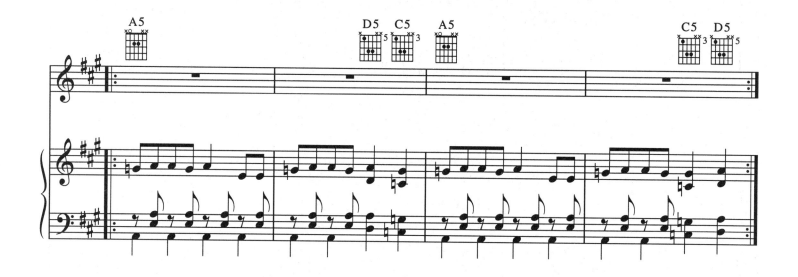

Verse 1:

1. When I die and they lay me to rest,___ gon - na go___ to the place___

Spirit in the Sky - 6 - 5
MFM0501CD

THE PRAYER

Italian Lyric by
ALBERTO TESTA and TONY RENIS

Words and Music by
CAROLE BAYER SAGER and DAVID FOSTER

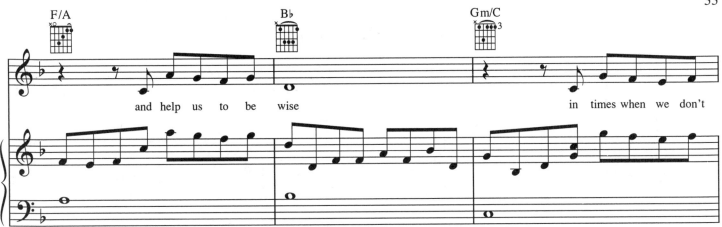

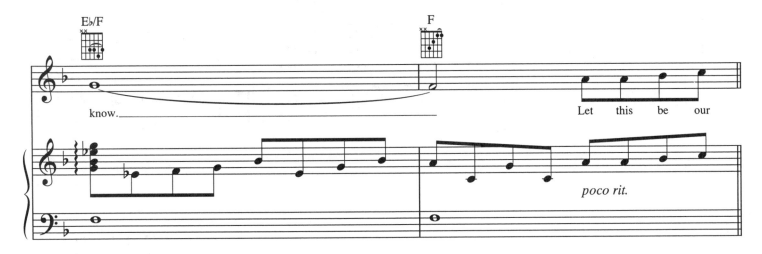

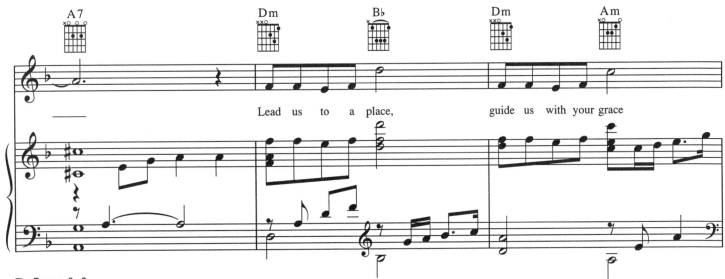

Verse 2:

THIS IS THE NIGHT

Words and Music by
CHRISTOPHER BRAIDE, GARY BURR
and ALDO NOVA

Slowly ♩ = 50

Verse 1:

1. When the world was-n't up-side down,___ I could

take all the time___ I had.___ But I'm not gon-na wait___ when a mo-

ment can van-ish so fast._____ 'Cause

This Is the Night - 6 - 1
MFM0501CD

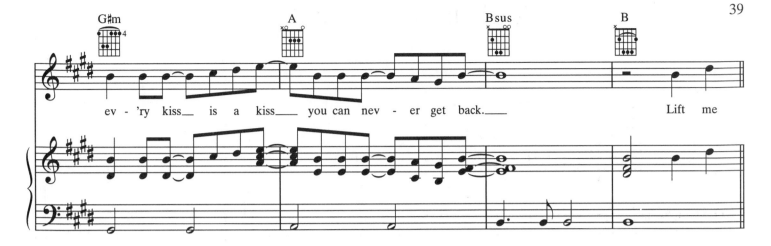

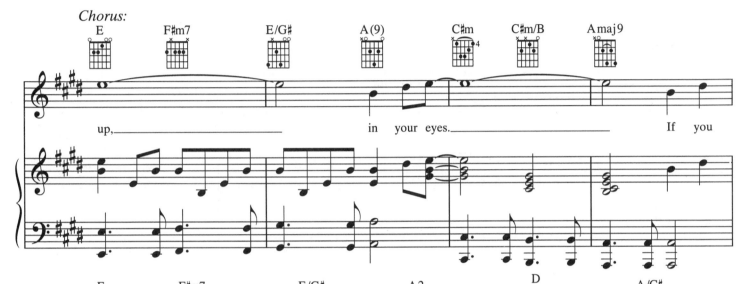

Chorus:

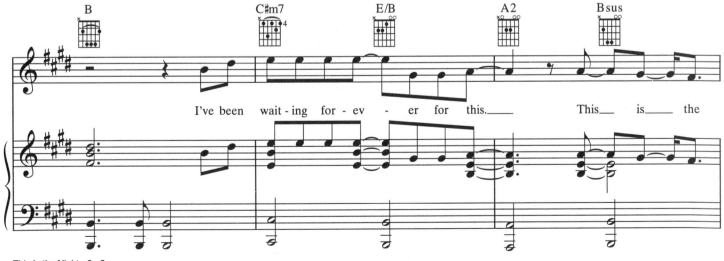

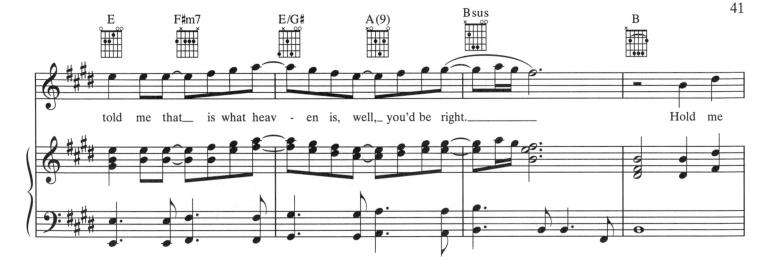

told me that is what heav - en is, well, you'd be right. Hold me

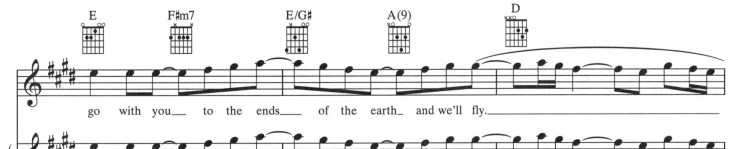

close to your heart. I would

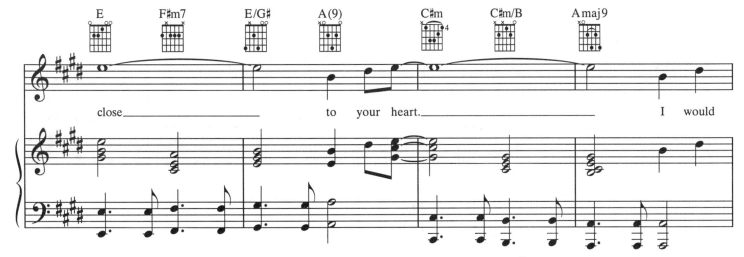

go with you to the ends of the earth and we'll fly.

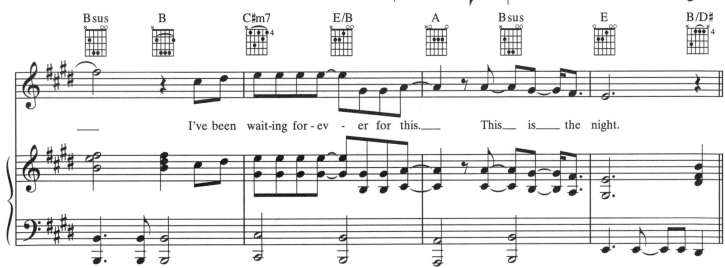

I've been wait-ing for - ev - er for this. This is the night.

WHAT ABOUT ME

Words and Music by
ALLAN FROST GARRY and
FRANCES CLAIRE SWAN

top. / stop.
He gets pushed a-round,__ / Well, she's not too proud__
knocked__ to the ground.__ / to__ cry out loud.__
He / She

gets to his feet and he says,__ / runs to the street and she screams,__
"What a-bout

Chorus:

me?__ It is-n't fair. I've__ had e-nough, now I

want my share.__ Can't you see__ I want to live? But

you just___ take___ more than you give."___ 2. Well, there's a

want to live? But you just___ take___ more than you

Bridge:

give." So take a step back and see the

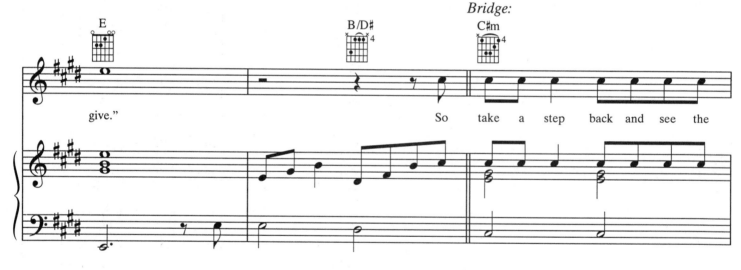

lit - tle peo - ple, the may be young but they're___ the ones who make the

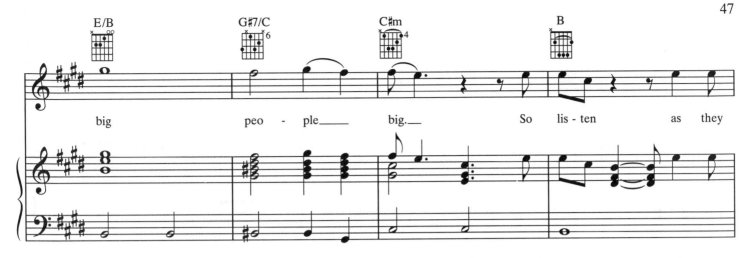

big peo - ple____ big.____ So lis - ten as they

Verse 3:

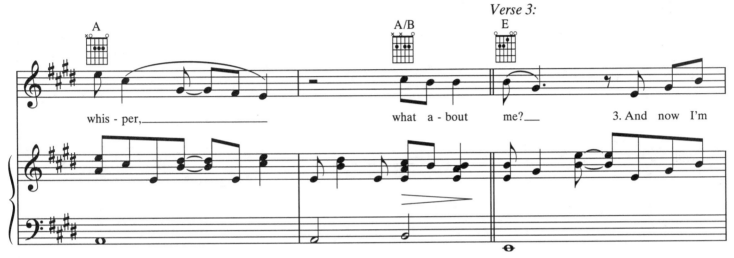

whis - per,_____ what a - bout me?____ 3. And now I'm

stand-ing on the cor - ner, all the worlds____ gone home.____ No -

bod - y's changed,____ no - bod - y's been saved and____ I'm feel - ing cold____

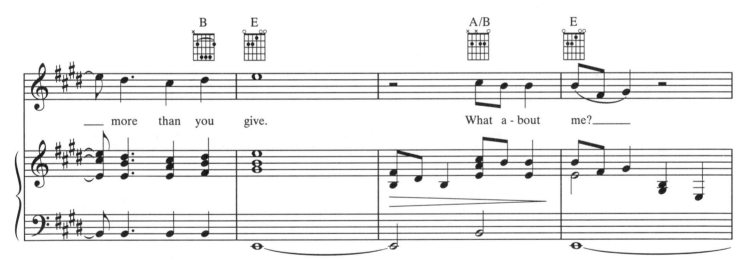

SUMMERTIME

By
GEORGE GERSHWIN,
DuBOSE and DOROTHY HEYWARD
and IRA GERSHWIN

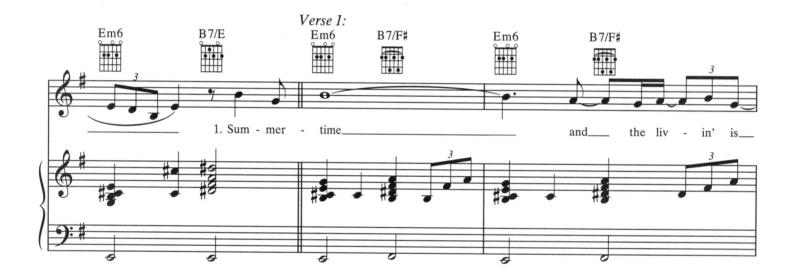

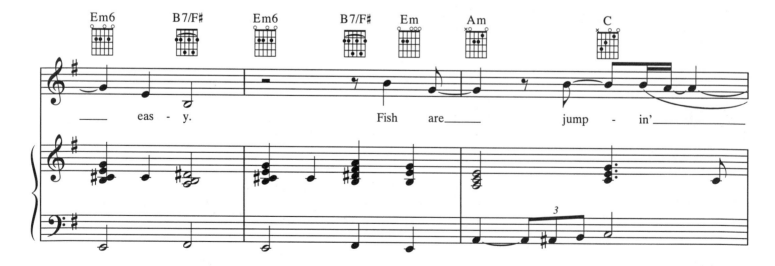

Verses 2 & 3:

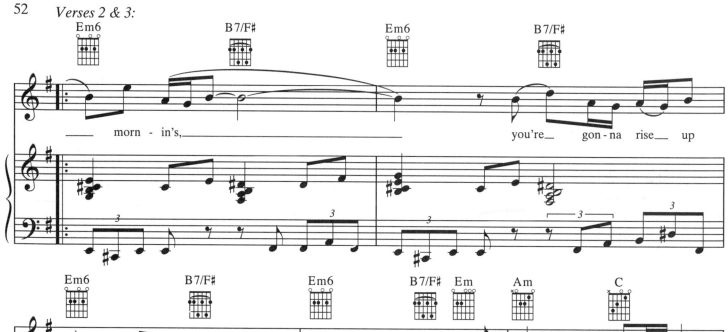

morn - in's,_____ you're__ gon - na rise__ up

sing - in'. Then you'll__ spread your__ wings_____

and__ fly to the sky._____ But till__ that__

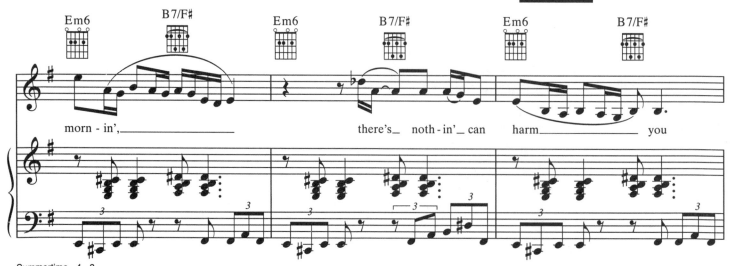

morn - in',_____ there's__ noth - in'__ can harm_____ you

The Collection Series

   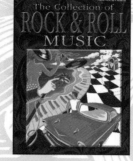 

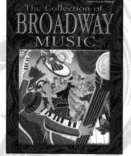 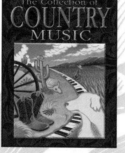

BIG BAND & BEYOND MUSIC
(MFM0406)
If you love that big band, can't get enough of that swing, and like to lounge around with the blues, this is *The Collection* for you. *Titles include:* Artistry in Rhythm • Drumboogie • Hallelujah! • I Gotta Right to Sing the Blues • It Don't Mean a Thing • The Lady Is a Tramp • Love Walked In • The Man I Love • Oh, Lady Be Good! • Swing Is Back in Style • This Can't Be Love • What's New, and many more.

BROADWAY MUSIC
(MFM0407)
All the best Broadway tunes are covered in this show-stopping collection. *Titles include:* And All That Jazz (*Chicago*) • Dancing Queen (*Mamma Mia!*) • Don't Rain on My Parade (*Funny Girl*) • Grease (*Grease*) • I Don't Know How to Love Him (*Jesus Christ Superstar*) • I Got Plenty o' Nuttin' (*Porgy and Bess*) • I Honestly Love You (*Boy from Oz*) • I've Got a Crush on You (*Strike Up the Band*) • People (*Funny Girl*) • Sunrise, Sunset (*Fiddler on the Roof*), and many more.

CLASSIC ROCK MUSIC
(MFM0402)
Get ready to rock with songs from the Eagles, Lynyrd Skynyrd, Van Morrison, and many more favorites. *Titles include:* After Midnight • Blinded by the Light • Dancing in the Dark • Go Your Own Way • Hotel California • I've Gotta Get a Message to You • Locomotive Breath • Moondance • Old Time Rock & Roll • Rock and Roll All Nite • Shake It Up • Sweet Home Alabama, and many more.

COUNTRY MUSIC
(MFM0403)
It's time to play your favorite country hits. *Titles include:* Amazed • Because You Love Me • Breathe • How Do I Live • I Like It, I Love It • I Will Always Love You • I'm Gonna Getcha Good! • It's Five O'Clock Somewhere • There's Your Trouble • Two Sparrows in a Hurricane • You're Still the One, and many more.

JAZZ MUSIC
(MFM0405)
In the mood for some jazz? This book's what you need! *Titles include:* As Time Goes By • Autumn Nocturne • Come Rain or Come Shine • 500 Miles High • Love for Sale • Lover Man (Oh, Where Can You Be?) • South Beach Mambo • That's All • Trav'lin Light • Witchcraft, and many more.

MOVIE MUSIC
(MFM0404)
Bring home the magic of the movies with this assortment of blockbusters. *Titles include:* Across the Stars (*Star Wars®: Episode II Attack of the Clones*) • All for Love (*The Three Musketeers*) • Because You Loved Me (*Up Close & Personal*) • Gollum's Song (*The Lord of the Rings: The Two Towers*) • How Do I Live (*Con Air*) • I Don't Want to Miss a Thing (*Armageddon*) • I Will Always Love You (*The Bodyguard*) • James Bond Theme (*Die Another Day*) • Stayin' Alive (*Saturday Night Fever*) • Theme from *Jurassic Park* • There You'll Be (*Pearl Harbor*), and many more.

ROCK & ROLL MUSIC
(MFM0408)
If you love that good old rock & roll, this collection has your favorite tunes. *Titles include:* Be My Baby • California Dreamin' • Da Doo Ron Ron • Great Balls of Fire • Hurt So Bad • I Want to Hold Your Hand • Itsy Bitsy Teenie Weenie Yellow Polka Dot Bikini • Let's Twist Again • (We're Gonna) Rock Around the Clock • Runaround Sue • Shake Rattle and Roll, and many more.

TV MUSIC
(MFM0409)
This book has all your new and old TV favorites. More than 90 of television's best themes including: 24 • Batman • Bonanza • Charlie's Angels • Everybody Loves Raymond • Hawaii Five-O • I'll Be There for You • Law and Order • The Pink Panther • The Rockford Files • Sex and the City • Song from M*A*S*H • The West Wing • Whose Line Is It Anyway, and many more.

WEDDING MUSIC
(MFM0401)
All the classical music favorites for the ceremony and popular love songs for the reception are in this great collection of wedding music. *Titles include:* Ave Maria (Bach/Gounod) • The Wedding March (from *A Midsummer Night's Dream*) • All the Way • Butterfly Kisses • Could I Have This Dance • Forever and for Always • From This Moment On • Here and Now • I Believe in You and Me • I Finally Found Someone • I Swear • I'll Always Love You • When I Fall in Love • With This Ring, and many more.

Printed in USA • AD0162B 5/04

THE SHEET MUSIC HITS SERIES

All Your Favorite Songs in Seven Music-Packed Volumes!

Popular Sheet Music Hits
(MFM0324)

Titles include: As Time Goes By • Back at One • Because You Loved Me • Foolish Games • God Bless the U.S.A. • Greatest Love of All • I Could Not Ask for More • I Turn to You • I Will Always Love You • Lean on Me • My Way • Now and Forever • Over the Rainbow • The Prayer • The Rose • Somewhere Out There • Theme from New York, New York • There You'll Be • A Thousand Miles • Time to Say Goodbye • To Where You Are • Un-Break My Heart • The Wind Beneath My Wings • You Needed Me • Your Song.

Country Sheet Music Hits
(MFM0322)

Titles include: Amazed • Because You Love Me • Breathe • Come On Over • Concrete Angel • The Dance • The Devil Went Down to Georgia • From This Moment On • Go Rest High on That Mountain • Holes in the Floor of Heaven • How Do I Live • I Could Not Ask for More • I Cross My Heart • I Hope You Dance • I Swear • I'll Be • I'm Already There • I'm Movin' On • The Keeper of the Stars • On the Side of Angels • Something That We Do • There You Are • This Kiss • When You Say Nothing at All • You're Still the One.

Classic Rock Sheet Music Hits
(MFM0323)

Titles include: After Midnight • American Pie • Aqualung • Bad Moon Rising • Black Water • Brown Eyed Girl • Down on the Corner • Drive • Europa • Free Bird • Gimme Some Lovin' • Go Your Own Way • Heart of Gold • Higher Love • Hotel California • Layla • Long Train Runnin' • Lyin' Eyes • Maggie May • Money • More Than a Feeling • Old Time Rock & Roll • Open Arms • Proud Mary • Sister Golden Hair • Someone Saved My Life Tonight • Truckin' • What a Fool Believes.

Movie Music Sheet Music Hits
(MFM0325)

Titles include: Somewhere Out There • Power of Love • The Entertainer • Stayin' Alive • It Might Be You • Because You Loved Me • That's What Friends Are For • As Time Goes By • How Do I Live • I Don't Want to Miss a Thing • A Fool in Love • There'll You'll Be • Come What May • Hedwig's Theme • In Dreams • Across the Stars • Fawkes the Phoenix • Gollum's Song • James Bond Theme • I Move On • Somewhere, My Love (Lara's Theme) • Over the Rainbow • Arthur's Theme • Eye of the Tiger • Wind Beneath My Wings.

TV Sheet Music Hits
(MFM0326)

Titles include: Batman • Boss of Me Now • ER (Main Theme) • Everybody Loves Raymond • Flying Without Wings • Hawaii Five-O • High Upon This Love • I'll Be There for You • Law and Order • Miami Vice • Mr. Ed • Nine to Five • The Pink Panther • Searchin' My Soul • Sex and the City • Song from M*A*S*H • Theme from Family Guy • Theme from Futurama • Theme from Magnum, P.I. • Theme from NYPD Blue • Theme from the Simpsons • This Is the Night • The West Wing • Where There Is Hope • Whose Line Is It Anyway? • Woke Up This Morning • Scooby-Doo (Main Theme) • Twilight Zone • Charlie's Angels • Theme from the X-Files.

Broadway Sheet Music Hits
(MFM0327)

Titles include: Almost Like Being in Love • And All That Jazz • Anything Goes • Beautiful City • Big Spender • Corner of the Sky • Dancing Queen • Don't Cry for Me Argentina • Embraceable You • Forty-Second Street • Good Morning Starshine • Heart • Hey There • I'll Never Fall in Love Again • I've Got a Crush on You • I've Gotta Be Me • Mack the Knife • New York, New York • On a Clear Day You Can See Forever • Ragtime • Send in the Clowns • Suddenly, Seymour • Summertime • Sunrise, Sunset • Thoroughly Modern Millie.

Wedding Sheet Music Hits
(MFM0328)

Titles include: All I Have • Always • Amazed • Because of You • Ave Maria (Schubert) • Endless Love • Bridal Chorus • At Last • Forever and for Always • From This Moment On • Here and Now • How Deep Is Your Love • I Swear • Love Like Ours • In Your Eyes • Once in a Lifetime • This Magic Moment • Tonight I Celebrate My Love • Wedding Song (There Is Love) • The Wedding March (from "A Midsummer Night's Dream") • With This Ring • Years from Here • You Light Up My Life • Your Love Amazes Me • You're the Inspiration.

Collect them all!

AD1132 11/03

100 years of Popular Music

Celebrate All the Classic Hits of the 20th Century with This New Series from Warner Bros. Publications

Eighty-nine hits from 1900 to 1920 in one collection! Aba Daba Honeymoon • Alexander's Ragtime Band • The Band Played On • A Bicycle Built for Two • Bill Bailey, Won't You Please Come Home? • Danny Boy • The Entertainer • Give My Regards to Broadway • Meet Me in St. Louis, Louis • Over There • Take Me Out to the Ball Game • When Irish Eyes Are Smiling • When the Saints Go Marching In • You're a Grand Old Flag, and many more.

1900 (MFM0306)

More than 250 pages of classic songs from the Roaring Twenties! Ain't We Got Fun • The Birth of the Blues • Bye Bye Blackbird • The Charleston • Clap Yo' Hands • Fascinating Rhythm • Get Happy • Hard-Hearted Hannah • I'm Just Wild About Harry • Ma! (He's Making Eyes at Me) • Makin' Whoopee! • Ol' Man River • 'S Wonderful • Singin' in the Rain • The Varsity Drag, and many more.

1920 (MFM0307)

A smokin' collection of favorites from the thirties! Ain't Misbehavin' • A-Tisket, A-Tasket • Begin the Beguine • Bei Mir Bist Du Schön • Embraceable You • A Fine Romance • Forty-Second Street • Hooray for Hollywood • I Got Rhythm • I've Got a Crush on You • Jeepers Creepers • Let's Call the Whole Thing Off • Lullaby of Broadway • My Heart Belongs to Daddy • Over the Rainbow • Summertime • The Way You Look Tonight, and many more.

1930 (MFM0308)

From the swingin' forties comes this incredible collection! Beat Me Daddy, Eight to the Bar • Bewitched • Body and Soul • Boogie Woogie Bugle Boy • Chattanooga Choo Choo • How High the Moon • I've Got a Gal in Kalamazoo • New York, New York • On Green Dolphin Street • Pennsylvania 6-5000 • 'Round Midnight • You Make Me Feel So Young, and many more.

1940 (MFM0309)

Catch all the smooth stylings and rock 'n' roll of the fifties! Blue Suede Shoes • Catch a Falling Star • Chances Are • Earth Angel • Enchanted • Good Golly Miss Molly • Great Balls of Fire • Mack the Knife • Only You (And You Alone) • Que Sera, Sera • (We're Gonna) Rock Around the Clock • Smoke Gets in Your Eyes • Splish Splash • Tammy • The Twelfth of Never, and many more.

1950 (MFM0310)

Collect all the soulful tunes of the sixties! Be My Baby • Brown-Eyed Girl • California Dreamin' • Chain of Fools • Crying • The Girl from Ipanema • I Say a Little Prayer • I Want to Hold Your Hand • It's Not Unusual • Let's Twist Again • Na Na Hey Hey Kiss Him Goodbye • Oh, Pretty Woman • Poetry in Motion • Proud Mary, and many more.

1960 (MFM0311)

Rock out with these great tunes from the seventies! All by Myself • American Pie • Can't Get Enough of Your Love, Babe • Dancing Queen • I Will Survive • If You Love Me (Let Me Know) • Killing Me Softly with His Song • Old Time Rock & Roll • Sister Golden Hair • Sweet Home Alabama • You're So Vain, and many more.

1970 (MFM0312)

All the unforgettable hits of the Me Decade! 1-2-3 • Addicted to Love • Arthur's Theme • Beat It • Call Me • Maneater • Morning Train (Nine to Five) • Owner of a Lonely Heart • The Safety Dance • She Works Hard for the Money • That's What Friends Are For • What's Love Got to Do with It • We Built This City • You Give Love a Bad Name, and many more.

1980 (MFM0313)

The hottest hits of the last decade! All for Love • All I Wanna Do • Believe • Dreaming of You • From This Moment On • Have I Told You Lately • Hold On • How Do I Live • I Will Always Love You • Insensitive • Ironic • Livin' la Vida Loca • Macarena • Save the Best for Last • Smooth • Stay (I Missed You) • Un-Break My Heart • Waiting for Tonight • Where Does My Heart Beat Now, and many more.

1990 (MFM0314)

All the modern hits of the new millennium so far! Bye Bye Bye • Can't Get You Out of My Head • Come on Over (All I Want Is You) • Complicated • Cry Me a River • Dilemma • Everywhere • Hero • Hey Baby • I'm Like a Bird • Love Don't Cost a Thing • Music • Show Me the Meaning of Being Lonely • Thank You • A Thousand Miles, and many more.

2000 (MFM0315)

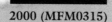

All editions are arranged for Piano/Vocal/Chords

AD1116 07/03